Catharsis
Journey of Emotional Healing

Aruna Murmu

BookLeaf Publishing

India | USA | UK

Presentation by *BookLeaf Publishing*

Web: www.bookleafpub.com

E-mail: info@bookleafpub.com

ISBN: 9789363317185

First edition 2024

I dedicate this book to my parents

Late Furmal Murmu

Mrs. Baso Murmu

ACKNOWLEDGEMENT

I acknowledge each and every individual who walked into my life. The good and bad are part of the journey but lessons learnt are priceless. Each individual adds meaning to my life in their own way. Some I lost along the way, some still with me in my journey.

PREFACE

"I know you're tired but come, this is the way." - Rumi

Life is shorter than we expect it to be. Dwelling in the past, harbouring grief, anger and pain in the present is unjustified to the self. It's like overburdening the self in the present that prevents us from experiencing joy. Resolve the conflict within, adapt means to heal and not let external factors steal the joy of being you.

Through this book, I aspire to reach especially women trapped in the confinement of their emotions. The only individual who will help you break the barrier is you and you alone. Hence, break free from negative thoughts by engaging in whatever you find joy in and move on in life.

TABLE OF CONTENTS

Family is all

Call them punching bags or bean bags to fall
upon
Literally family is all one can think of
When backbreaking burdens dampen your spirits
It's family holding you from shattering to pieces
Backbone of our lives
In rain and sunshine, they help us thrive

The world will judge you anyways
Happy to leave you with bruises
The entire race that you chase
Nothing new if you lose
All that matters is how you face
The challenges that leave you ablaze

The family does have senses
They notice however small changes
Physical emotional conditional

Make yourself approachable
Open up to family,
They will neither judge nor put you on the edge

Life goes on with no replay
Making memories on the way
Nothing is here to stay
Parents age and wither away
Siblings grow and get separated
The bitter truth, we take family for granted.

Home is where the heart is

Built with bricks and mortar
Invisible blood and sweat
From a bachelor to a couple
Growing into a family of seven
What the world calls a house
We call it home

From changing wall colours
To modifying interior decors
This home has warmth love and care
Kindness in abundance to share
Small silly fights and accomplishments
The four walls witnessed all moments

Candles blown and birthdays celebrated
Siblings growing in inches and kgs
Watching our parents grow old
Like a river that has flowed its course
Tears of joy and sorrow
Dad's leaving left a huge hollow

Thirty years to build this home
With beautiful garden in full bloom
And courtyard for granddaughter to play
Laughter and giggles everyday
It feels like a payday
For what we built till date

Mentally straining emotionally challenging
It is to vacate this place
Dad's struggle Mom's cuddle
Pleasant memories to behold
What to collect? What not to collect?
For this home has our heart.

A sincere apology

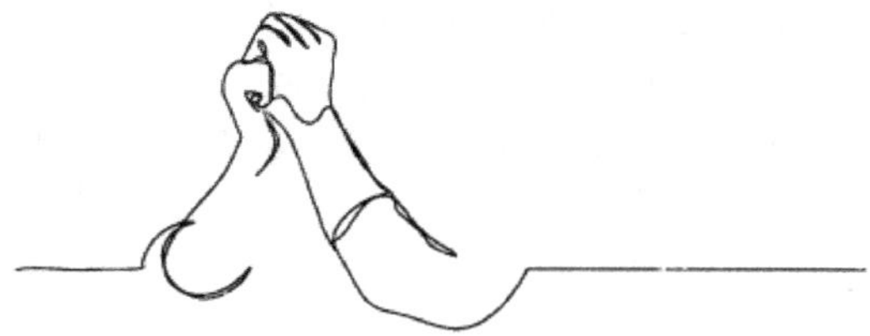

Hey dear little sister
Wish I could tell you
How ashamed I am of self
To have jeopardised your existence
Burdened you with responsibilities
That I was supposed to shoulder accountability

Wish I could tell you my side of the story
I was paying heavy price for the position that
looked rosy
I felt defeated, ethically, morally, financially and
emotionally
Projects failed collaborations lost
Years of hard work only to exhaust

I was bankrupt financially and emotionally
With nothing to give, I walked down the aisle
In hope of support that I can cling to
Little did I know then, we would fall apart
The shoe I was supposed to wear
You would have to force it through.

I had loved you and I still love you
I was there for you and will be in future too
Just that, now I am misunderstood
My genuine gestures misinterpreted
I offer help as family
But you refuse to take any

Forgive me for my mistakes
I realise it and concede
Blood relations cannot be broken
For such connections are made from heaven
Look forward to keeping your ego aside
Grateful that we are blessed to have each other.

Prayer to be heard

Going through the clutter
I could feel my heart flutter
Found a piece of paper in trash
Years of struggle faintly flashed
Desperate prayer scribbled on a page
Trying to break through the mental cage

I read the resentment of leaving a job
Pain of parting ways from love
The grudge held against family
Covid lockdown added to insanity
Tough survival away from home
We could witness withdrawal syndrome

Now I understand the physical behaviour
Of someone looking up to me as a saviour
The irritation and frustrations bottled up
Hopelessness and depression killing joy
Stone cold hearted she pretended to be
With soul wrecking storm ravaging within

I read in astonishment word by word
Getting to know the struggle unheard
The guilt of ignorance seeped in
Was naïve to understand my own kin
The letter left me feeling bleak
With tears rolling down my cheeks.

Blissful days

Grief-stricken we all were
Yet smiles and happy faces galore
Surviving through dark days
I know how I dealt with losing my dad

I was the first to be told
What the near future was to hold
With folded hands and head hung in prayer
I cried my heart away in despair

Facing my dad felt bitter and cheated
He sensed my quietness and asked my mom
"What is it that I secretly hold?"
Faked a smile and assured him all was good

Lying is tough yet we lied to a dying man
Gave him hope that it will be all fine
The vibes were cold
And worries overshadowed the calm

We packed our bags and travelled home
Along the journey we could see him lost
Friends and family were all informed
To visit my dad when still around

Glimmering lights lit up the earth
My dad hanging on to his flickering life
The day we dreaded finally arrived
He didn't witness post-diwali dawn

Grief-stricken we stood by each other
The emptiness we experienced was a nightmare
Losing a father was not just another loss
We found ourselves lost and shattered

Managing loss in our own ways
With unanswered questions still in mind
A decade later we still strive for normalcy
Reminiscing and exclaiming
Blissful days with little resources.

Diwali : A hindu festival of Lights.

Everlasting longing

Meet me at the horizon
At the valley of flowers
Where flowerbed kisses the sky
 In the midst of the endless ocean
Boats sailing with flickering lights
In peace and tranquillity
Where we have each other to hold
Countless unsaid stories to be told
Of everything that happened after you
Granddaughter fondly remembering you
Her complaints whispered in your ears
Seeking blessings for all our endeavours
Feeling you in every old man we see
Assuming how our life would have been
We long to meet you, dear papa
To let you know how much we loved you
And missed you each day in these years
Fondly remembering you with smiles and tears.

They them theirs

I am I, and nobody can be me
I may be tall or short in height
Big or small by built
White or brown in colour
Large, medium or small by size
How does it matter to you?

When I was skinny, they said
Your mother doesn't feed you well
When I put on weight, they said
Eat a little less, you are getting fat
Now that I am fit and healthy, they say

Why do you workout so much?
Quick are they to comment
"Oh! Maintaining your sexy figure."
How insensitive of them to body shame
With remarks, nonsense and lame.

I have come to realise lately
Why empower people to belittle you
Reacting to everything said and argue
Accept self in all its virtue
Ignore the negatives and shut them up
They, them, theirs are mere scrub.

Amorous More

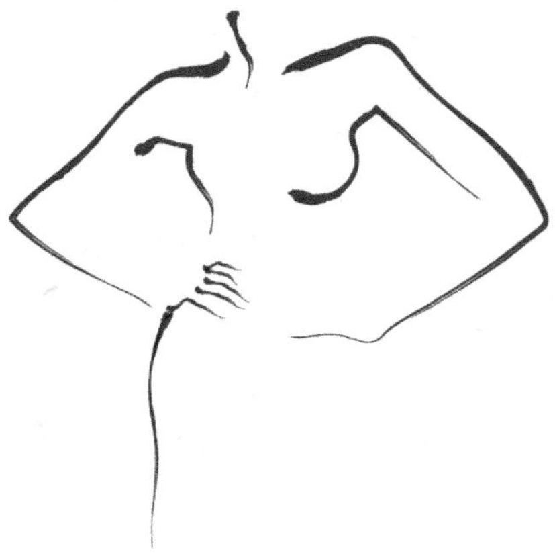

I am no special,
Yet I get your attention

I have no clue
What attracts you?

I am older I say
But in your opinion I slay

With kids I am married
You say you aren't worried

I say you are late
You say it's ok to date

You don't seem sophy
To ask me for coffee

This game is no fun,
As I am always on the run

Please stop this chase
I have some grace

I found my love,
That fits me like a glove

Be a man of substance
Don't prove your incompetence

Women aren't objects
That you treat with disrespect

Hope you mend your ways
It'll bring you disgrace.

Tagged

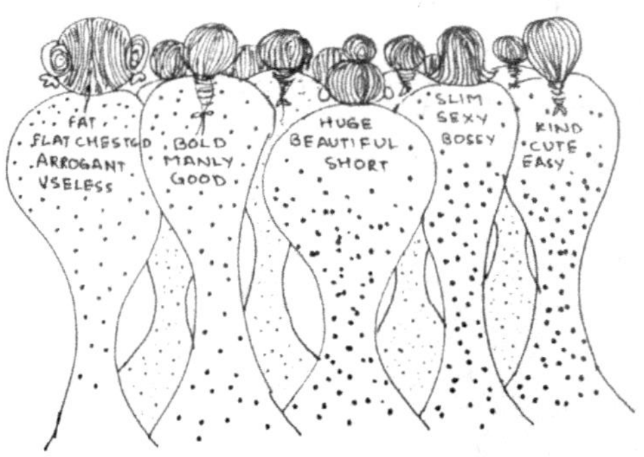

Commodities have tags
Do humans have tags too?
Maybe; maybe not?
But I have been tagged,

She's rude and snobby
She's arrogant
She's aggressive
She's loud
She's opinionated
She's unapologetic
She's stubborn
She's a pain in the ass

Alas,
None of these said to my face
Guess they didn't have the courage
I never took it to heart

Shrugged it off with a shrug
What's the fun in being everyone's apple pie?
When I add so many flavours.

The fight that it was

One important thing I learnt in life was to fight
And fight when someone is still alive

I fought for commitment
I fought for togetherness
I fought for inclusion
I fought for acceptance
I fought for my insecurities
I fought to hold you back
I fought for all things unseen and unheard

I had lost a battle before
One that shattered me from within
One that shook me to the core

One that I couldn't defy
It was losing my dad
It was the day I realised what love is
As I stared for him to open his eyes
As I laid my ears to hear his heartbeat
Held his hands to hold me back
I knew how much I fought
To not let him slip by
But painful it was to kiss goodbye

That was a day and this is another
I respect your choices and decisions
No explanation needed or to be given
So I set you free my dear
Free from my expectations
I set you free from me
And declare, the fight that it was is finally over.

Bemoans

My regrets are bigger than your presence in my
life
No, I mean it, as I have seen it
From drowning in liquor to infidelity as a
winner
You spread a platter of all you had to offer

Tarnishing my image to console your ego
Making me feel inadequate mocking my
individuality
Cussing my mother and my siblings
You found utterly fulfilling
I worked you lamented your exes worked you
applauded

Explaining how this marriage works
Women stay home while men run errands

Gradually I comprehend what you wanted
A nanny to look after you and a maid to clean
your house
Stern with food choices
A cook to provide sumptuous meals
Sorry to disappoint, yes I am disappointing and
hopeless
I couldn't trim your dirt-clogged nails
Or file your dusty dry chapped feet
Neither am I good at cooking and cleaning
Nor am I good at taking orders
I am a homewrecker as your sister defines
Financing her home I refuse to be fine

Whatever names you may call me
I call it self care and guarding my peace
Of course, I regret this phase of my life
And my regrets are bigger than your presence in
my life.

Didn't your mother teach you?

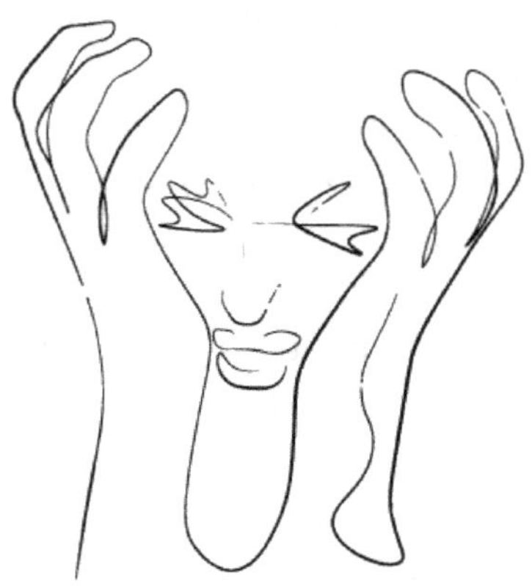

I didn't know I was inadequate, until I got
married
Into an affluent family, who boasts of being
moneyed?
A girl from a middle-class family
Brought up disciplined and omniscient
Where morals and ethics are valued
At my in-laws I constantly hear
"Didn't your mother teach you?"

I look around and see my spouse
Stress seems to automatically lessen
Poor fellow can't do a thing

Can't pour tea without a spill
I wonder if he has any skill
I guess he wasn't taught anything either
An individual vehemently clueless and crazier

Accustomed to taunts at in-laws' place
I take it sportingly and find solace
I'll learn the lurks and perks
And get away with scornful remarks
My mother may have taught me, more than
You taught your son, but in your opinion
"My mother will have never taught me
anything."

Women of substance

A well-wisher a progressive male
Would like to see you do well
In all aspects of life,
From professional to personal
I wonder who he was?
The one I called my supervisor
My principal investigator, my mentor
I suppose mentor does mentoring
Supervising mentees to their destination

My whole career I had a male mentor
The one who undervalued my efforts
And unappreciated my skills
Maybe I wasn't up to the mark

Or didn't have all it takes to remark
I was discouraged each day at work
Accepted his attitude as little quirks
What offset them is still unknown
But they stole my work as I reckon
Ripped me off my credentials
To publish in high-impact journals
When I protested, was shown the door
Who knows what happens behind closed doors?

Some women manipulated data
Some women manipulated the people
Some women manipulated the boss
Some women resorted to sugary words
It was a realm of perform or perish
Nothing short of nightmarish
It was a race to excel
Only if you succeed to impress the mentor
Because mentor was not just a mentor
But a way to jobs and opportunities
Favouritism took over excellence
And claim, they make women of substance.

Live Love Laugh

Bitterness overshadowed the goodness in me
Allowing the world to modulate to a degree
I was bruised, cheated and played on
Succumbed to storm that outweighed me
Those weren't uneducated labour class
So-called academicians' intellectuals high class
They had a lot at stake, name, fame and respect
They forget every individual has self respect
The experiences are for a lifetime
We need to make them count
Today I call it past
But the hurt was there to last
The price I paid was hefty
Not just professional
Emotional, mental and physical
For years I went through hell
Practising self-awareness to come out of shell
Every cloud has a silver lining

Accepting self and mindful learning
To live every moment, love much and laugh
often.

Baggage claim

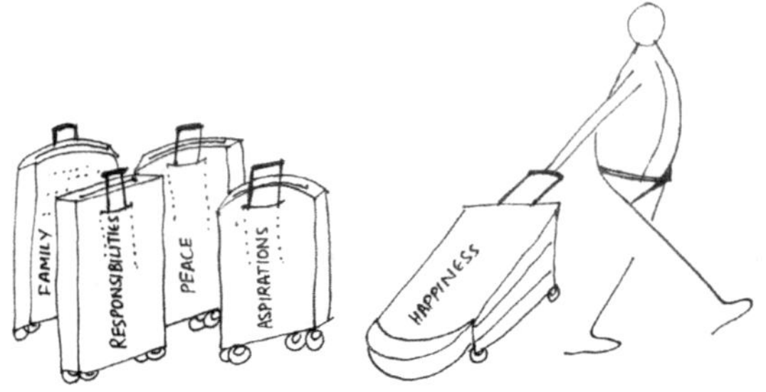

Some baggage's need not be claimed
And nobody to be blamed
We aren't programmed to let it go
Neither to take a 'No' or say 'No'
Family's expectation
Friends' admiration
Our aspiration
Self-validation
Prosperous life manifestation
Neighbours' comparison
We live in this loop
Till our spirits droop
We need to tag our baggage
Priority or trivial
Relevant or unimportant
And not lose self in the moment
Let it go if it needs to
Hold to choices that nourish you

A company that flourishes you
Memories that you will cherish
Drop baggage that leaves you in anguish.

A girl is born

The world might have said
Mirthlessly, "it's a girl"
But for my parents, we were their cosmos

Grandma wanted another boychild
Hence we were born five
My parents found it special
Bringing up five kids tested their mettle
With no gender discrimination
We witnessed the magic of nurturance

I sometimes wonder,
Each girl child born, is already a race won
Because everyone prayed for son
Societal norms aren't fair either
Dictating every feminine behaviour

Sit like this, talk like that
Behave like this and what not?
Irrespective of gender bias and societal
limitation
We exist, excel and lead by example
Be as daughters, wives or mothers.

Once in a blue moon

Once in a blue moon,
You show up from nowhere
Time and again in these years
Not for me, but for yourself

Cherishing the good times we shared
Longing to meet one last time
Away from the hustle and bustle of city life
In peace and tranquillity

It's been ages we burnt the bridge
Holding no regrets or grudges
I closed this book long ago, yet I wonder
What brings you back to me?

For me, that one last time was our last meeting
Heartbroken and unhappy, I was left reeling
Relationship terms and conditions disclosed
Unfortunately, no conclusions reached

You left to pursue your ambitions
To far faraway land
With different time zone and new set of friends
Our journey was meant to end

Months passed without communication
And soon it turned into years
In our lives we paved our own ways
Feelings and emotions obscured in haze

With a wonderful man holding my hand
Time slipped away like grains of sand
With innumerable joyful memories to behold
Loved and accepted the way I am

Irrespective of endless convincing done
To meet up one last time for fun
Since circumstances have changed since then
I am unwilling to walk that dreaded path again

Don't show up when you are lonely
Or when you need a shoulder to cry
A lovable faithful companion is a bliss
Yet your well being is all I wish

In silence

I left the place I didn't belong
Where staying longer felt wrong
Heated argument behind closed doors
I couldn't ignore anymore

They talked their share of the story
Sipping coffee and speaking softly
Discussing me in all possible ways
That continued for days

Guessing my views and opinions
On gossip, they needed to listen
I did not want to lose my peace
After all, I have endured for long

Made up my mind to declare
And embrace growth in near future
Signing contract and resigned
Leaving the people and belongings behind

I left the place without a single word
And they haven't heard from me till date
Silence speaks a thousand words
I hope my message was clear and loud.

Friendship with no clause

I was an obedient daddy's girl
Yet he sent me away
It was raining heavily that day
With my belongings and nothing to say
We waited for kids to return from school
Daddy signed the admission form
To find myself in the dorm
With kids around
Parents nowhere to be found
Gradually the days went past
Homesickness crept fast
Silently weeping, wetting the pillow
Questioning my daddy from hostel window
Years passed by with friends by my side
With whom life updates I could share
From having a crush to going on a date
We contemplate, communicate and celebrate
Meet up once in a while
Filling the room with smile

Never feels like meeting after ages
As we embrace inner changes
Fortunate to have this connection
Where we can be us without tension.

Nora; the quirky Dora

I have a dear friend named Nora
No less than the character Dora
Cute little girl with beautiful hair
She indeed hid many layers
Humorous, naughty, curious teenager
Anecdotes to remember forever

Warden was always confused
Nora Aruna Aruna Nora, till they get used
To differentiate between the two
They needed to know who's who
Unevenly chopping friends' hair
Hiding to evade the angry stare
Exchanging jam for auto fare
Many stories I have to share
Bunk school without breaking the rule
yet get good score
Sherlock Holmes and Nancy Drew

Her mind always had mischief to brew
Unexpected unheard tales of Nora
We aptly call her "The Quirky Dora."

Love yourself

The magic of self-love is mesmerising
It waters your soul and spirit
And transforms your lifeless life
It gives you purpose
And reminds to work on self relentlessly

The world becomes a better place
When you learn to love self first
You can only give when you have an abundance
A broken heart cannot love
A broken soul cannot motivate
A broken spirit cannot uplift

To serve others mend self first,
be it family or friends
The day you put yourself together,
 is the day you are reborn
To shine and conquer,
marching on with shining armour

Self-love is liberating,
Opens possibilities captivating
It frees your mind of negatives
Takes you on ventures unimagined

Smile is all she could borrow

Soothing smiling faces
We all like to embrace
The vibrancy, the aura
That leaves you enchanted
Living up to her name
Compounding fragrance with her presence

Perfect life often attracts evil eyes
Married at eighteen widowed at thirty
Loneliness wrecks the human within
Yet living in a mundane
Not crying over spilled milk
Or playing the blame game

The enchanting smile that we see
Is expensive I guarantee
For we will never know

Countless battles the soul has won
In moments of sorrow
Smile is all she could borrow.

Healing

Ever wondered what healing looks like?
I met one and hence I know

A healed individual doesn't react
Instead responds sensibly and enact
The external murmur bothers less
Existing to be happy and no one to impress
The anxiety taken over by calmness
Focus shifted towards self-progress
Prioritises health and be an inspiration
Without seeking any external validation
Radiating positivity wherever they are
Emotionally stable to be own guiding star

Ambitious with clarity of mind
Leaving the agony behind

Cool composed personalities aren't to be
confused
For they are tough to be pursued
Humble and grounded, empathetic and kind
Been through purgatory, emerging refined
Harping on moral values, seeking spirituality
Invested in the present, living in reality.
These are a few traits I see in me
From the shackles of the past, I set myself free.

Take the leap again

I get tired too
Mentally, physically, emotionally
Take a step back and reset
Before I take the leap again

Rejuvenated restarted all over again
New identity itched to my name
Not the degree or the recommendation
Persistence paved the way for buried passion

Sat long enough staring at the closed door
Now I anticipate what's in the store
Explore self and the world around
Rise to the challenge with joy profound

As I age I learned it the hard way
My peace is not trivial to be given away
Hence, I left all that didn't add value
Be it people, places and jobs that rue

Life lately has been slow
Unmatched beneficence at the fore
Gratitude and satisfaction are my prize
For not letting myself down in my eyes.

Kindness goes a long way

Swollen eyes and gloomy face
I have been watching her for few days
Couldn't resist myself further
Hence approached with no intention to hurt her
Seems she's been troubled for days
Hence tears rolled down her cheeks

Unwilling to open up to me, I didn't force her
either
I asked her to cry her heart out
Made her understand that she is important
Worries are part of life and life goes on
Everyone you see around has problems in life
Some fixable while some out of our hands
Why worry about something beyond our control
Believe in God and he will do his best

Gradually she calmed down
Wiped tears off her cheeks

A resilient smile adorned her lips
And we were good to go
Life is better if we observe around
Kindness and empathy don't cost much
Yet these gestures go a long way.

Of becoming

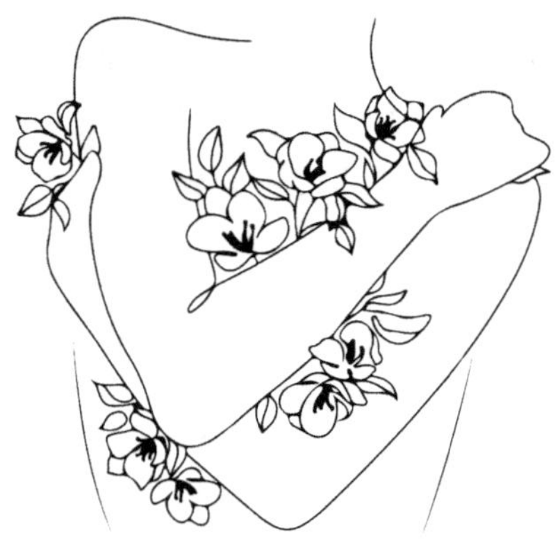

I am tough and hard on self sometimes
But I can be nice and silly too
The people's perception of me is deceptive
When I get to know I laugh out loud
Because I don't recognize the person they
describe
I remember as a kid I was too shy and
introverted
Barely speaking, forget the expression of
thoughts
I did admire the girls around
Who were boisterous and expressive
Who knew their choices, be it trifle as
What's their favourite food or how they liked to
dress

Clear in vision of what they want in life
I was amazed and wanted to be one of them
Ages passed and life was no less than a roller
coaster
I realised if you don't speak up you are taken for
granted
So I improved my communication skills
It's so needed to voice your views and opinions
So I preferred to be well-informed about the
world around me
It's so needed to have a mind of your own
Ability to analyze and express your views
I now know my favourite food
And what is my comfort attire to adorn
I now know I am important
Even if the world doesn't pay heed
I learned to love myself more than ever
When I look back
I absolutely love who I have become.

Banyan tree

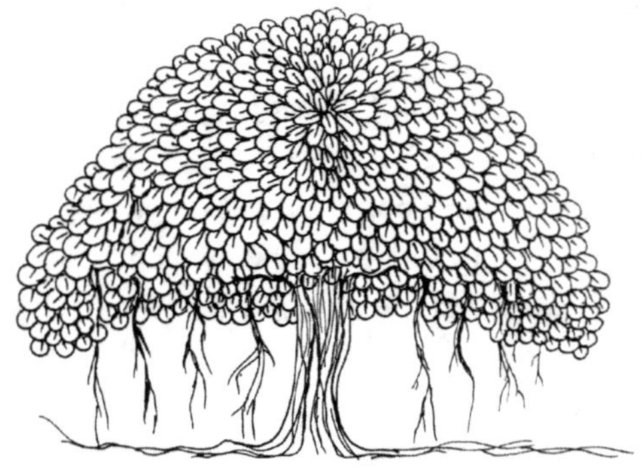

You stood here for ages
With generations playing under your shade
Ladies and kids enjoying swings
Singing melodious tunes
Kids climbing your branches
And shaking you up
I wonder, if you are tickled
And enchanted by melodies like we do

Do you feel us too?
You have witnessed so many
Stories, sad and happy
Of my fathers and forefathers
Wish you had a voice so that
Anyone coming to you
Get to hear your stories
I am fascinated; you still exist in your glory

Whereas I have grown old
With golden hair and wrinkles

I wonder,
While I am gone someday
My kids will play under your shade
Looking up to you in joy
Swinging from your branches
In the summer afternoon
Ladies chatting and laughing away
Sharing stories of their lifetime
While you stand by them
For generations to come.

Summer holidays

Summers are here so are the holidays
Destination holidays? Who cared then
Our ultimate destination was grandparents'
home
With aunts and uncles around
Home buzzing with warmth and joy
Abundant pampering and cajoling
Is what made up our summer holidays

Climbing trees, plucking mangoes
A bit of salt and chilly to tango
We ran around in mirth and joy
Secretly buying snacks to enjoy
Paddy fields ploughed for monsoon
Enjoying food in the fields
An experience worth a lifetime to cherish

Soon the monsoon arrives
Watering million lives and hopes
Pleasant breeze and rain-washed earth
Ponds and lakes overflowing
Kids out swimming, fishing and playing
Earth smiling so were we
And just like that it was time to leave

Luggage was packed, loaded with gifts
Leaving refreshed and uplifted
Summer holiday at grandparents' was blissful
As we grew older, summer holidays became rare
Consumed by tutions and examinations
Adulthood only expanded our limitations.

Pandemic blues

While the world was locked up globally
Humanity was put to test amicably
Life is shorter than we think
Is what epidemic taught us on the brink

With lives lost each second
We checked on with forgotten loved ones
Work from home became a new norm
Feeling the pressure to perform

For those staying away from home
Maggie was up for the rescue
Indoor workouts became a trend
Marriage was virtually attended

Safe at home binged on Netflix shows
Glance at news brought emotional woes
Non-conventional means to procure vaccination
During this time were numerous innovations

Masked up to avoid infection
Using sanitizer in every situation
Coronavirus, RTPCR, Immunity and
Vaccination
The severity of viral infection was beyond
imagination

Though our lives were put on pause
Break from the rat race we gained perspectives
On life, love, money and relationships
Gratitude that we survived the phase

Walk of serenity

Finally, the monsoon arrived after a long wait
this year
Rain splashing on the windowpane is soothing to
ear
People enjoying the rains with near and dear
ones
Can see my neighbours with chai and maska bun

Waterfalls pouring down from hills a little far
Dark clouds approaching as I see from afar
Suited up in raincoats, kids ready to drench
Elderly with umbrellas seated on the park bench

Sitting on the balcony I watch the world around
me
Everything moving from leaves to water, except
me
Even the creek water changed in few hours
What am I? A dry log or an alive human being

Ashamed of self I decided to take a walk down
Wrapped in raincoat I walked slowly in lown
The longer I walked the harder was the
downpour
Whoever said 'rain infuses life' was true to its
core

'Why am I cold-hearted?' is what I asked self
While the world is brimming with limitless
emotions
Why do I restrict myself from opening up?
Pondering as I walked in the rain

Smiling I took the road home
Finding serenity as rain washed away my
gloominess
Rain brought clarity to thoughts that consumed
me
I experienced the joy of being free just as the
kids did.

Hostel days

Hostel life was so much fun
The first day was always tears and gloom
The joy of meeting old friends and
Taking notice of new faces in the dorm

Soon the routine hostel life resumes
With morning cringing wake-up bell
Scheduled study hours and playtime
To fixed menu on the dining table

Saturdays were designated cleaning days
From toilets to diner to dorm to study
Cleaning blocked sewer to cutting the
overgrown grass
In monsoon, we picked snails with bare hands

Sundays were a bit relaxing
Yummy breakfast and sumptuous lunch
Sunday mass and shows to binge
A happy vibe with parents around

Secretly plucking mangoes and guavas
The washer man's bicycle rides in pyjamas
Afternoon tuitions for extra fun
Warden's caning on scoring low

Permission to visit market was rarely granted
Dhokla and chicken rolls were secretly sneaked
Movie time and picnics were eagerly awaited
And Holi celebrations were awfully dreaded

We weren't allowed to speak to boys
Yet few of us secretly had a crush
Evening tea on terrace, simultaneously
Eyeballing on handsome guys

Carefree we lived far away
Amongst friends that were like family
We laughed and mocked our hostel days
Indeed those were the golden childhood days.

Memories

Found an old file from a decade ago
A file of images when we were naïve and young
I looked at myself and felt foolish
Dangling earrings and high heels
Long black hair and a bright red dress
Alas, knowledge and wisdom do have grace
Pictures of rumoured couples
Of colleagues and good friends

Relationships are delicate is what I learned
The best friends who were like shadow
Their promises proved to be shallow
Each association measured in terms and
conditions
Competitiveness was put before friendship
Ethically incorrect breaching of trust
Unbothered to be morally wrong
As long as the goals were achieved

Some faces were genuine and truthful
Simple outside, simpler inside
One pure soul we lost too soon
Calm, soft-spoken with a radiant smile
Pictures of a young and lively bunch
Leaving an impression from Harvard to Yale
Some personalities were strong-headed
They went on to pave their own ways

Complexities are disturbing
Be it friendship, love or marriage
In those images, I saw complexity
Of raw emotions and relationships
That felt superficial and artificial
Scrolling the files, only to realise
I had captured the transient associations
And blurred memories for the life

Imperfections

I knew a man who lived a lie
A lie he could easily deny
Known to get hopelessly inebriated
Being confronted was what he absolutely hated

A girl walked into his life
With hopes and dreams, best known as his wife
The union seemed unmatched
With speculations it won't survive

The wife observed him to later mention
The habits were beyond comprehension
Pushing the wife towards depression
Any intervention caused unneeded tension

The glass bottles stacked over time
And she beautifully painted them all
Painting roses and daisies with twinkling vine
In the chaos she chose to shine

With marriages crumbling around
Like a pack of cards
Not of strangers but family and friends
This marriage survived the wrath of time

It looked all lovey-dovey and spiced up
It's a mystery whether they were in love
Their secret recipe for being together
They learned to live with each other's
imperfections.

Acceptance

I accepted myself the way I am
Half of my problems were solved
I learned to own my flaws
And I never felt so liberated
I prayed for circumstances beyond my control
And he rightfully showed me the way
I accepted my mistakes
Never to repeat again, and I felt light
I owned my decisions and choices
When regret consumed my heart and mind
I accepted that I wasn't the best
For all the rejections I received
I accepted I needed to change my profession

And I found my passion
I accepted I needed to believe in myself
And I found my dreams turn into reality
I accepted that I needed to be happy
And I found the peace of mind
I am learning, learning each day
From people and places and everything around
But above all, I learned that
Acceptance does empower you.

Self worth

One day you finally realise
Your self-worth does matter
And no one can turn around your life
Unless you learn to fight
Fight your demons
Fear, insecurities and if's and but's
Fight the voices that deter you
And fuel your doubts
Sometimes it boils down to self
Because you know your self worth.

Gymtimidation

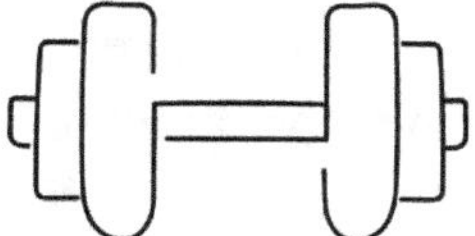

When the whole class jeered at me
Fat Shaming in unison
M.O.T.I here comes MOTI
It never bothered me nor was I hurt
Until I literally weighed heavy
And I was genuinely fat

Walked into gym, to shed some pounds
With eyes glued on me, I slightly frowned
Wobbly belly cried to be dressed appropriately
Looking for hideouts to exercise secretly
Gel-set hair and toned muscled trainers
Not to lie I was genuinely traumatised

Shed four pounds from grind of a month
Longing for abs I continued doing crunch
Puma Adidas Nike Reebok, looking for latest
fashion
Purchased new clothes, in search of motivation
Read gym quotes, to fire the desire
To look like those, toned models on cover

Rolling eyes do bother
Especially from the young guys who hover
Oldies aren't less either
With sceptical look and judgemental stares
You can sense the vibes around
Of guys trying to leave an impression

I was intimidated as a newbie
Not to deny I hated the ogling eyes
That makes you conscious
Of thick hips and heavy breasts
However decent you dress
None is spared from the penetrating stares.

Moti: Slang used to address a bulky individual.

Longing

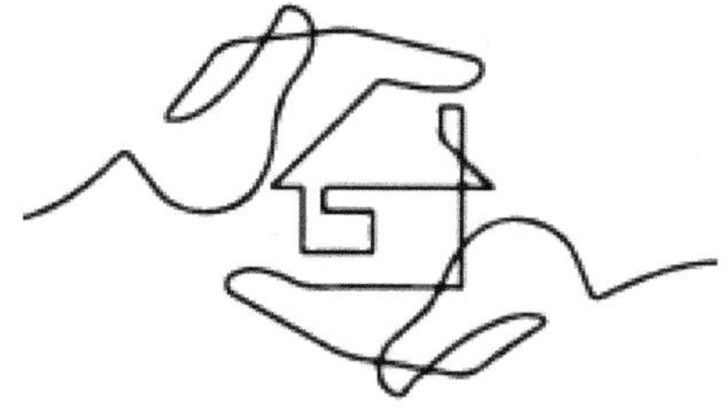

My heart longs for a house I can call home
That I can decorate according to my likes
Hang my beautiful paintings on the east-facing
wall
A touch of colour here and there, a bohemian
feel
Have a beautiful garden with roses and
sunflowers
With ivy and bluebells blooming on arched
gateway

My job is tricky as it takes me places
Temporary abode makes me feel like a wanderer
However hard I try,
The space misses the sense of belonging
Governed by tenure and office orders
I write chapters to remember.

Loving, sharing and caring

I stopped complaining
Because the joy is lost
And practised gratitude
For blessings I am gratified
Lord has given me all I need
And share what I have bountiful
Kindness in today's world
Easily misinterpreted and misunderstood
Suspicion overcomes the gesture
Of loving, sharing and caring.

Reserved

"Don't talk to me" is my armour
Until I am sure of you
You may call me arrogant
But you need to be relevant
I am not shy or anti-social
I am present and observing
Small talks aren't interesting
What's the point of pretending?
To unwillingly be part of a crowd
Yet finding yourself secluded
Discuss sports, politics and science
And whatever comes to mind
But not acquaintances to malign

With satirical jokes to talk behind
Don't embarrass me in public
Or taunt me for being reserved
If I open myself to you
Consider yourself someone dear.

My daughter

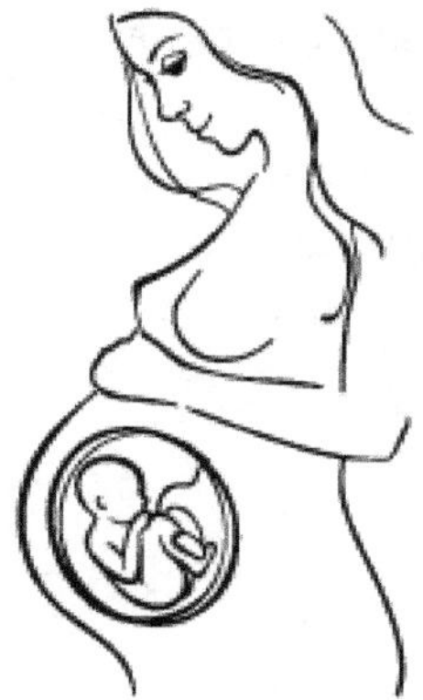

If I ever have a child
I want it to be a girl child
I will protect her at all cost
From being lost

To the cruel standards and norms
The society has laid for us women
Her identity, her individuality
Will be all hers

Without needing to emulate
Either of her parents
Or need any comparisons
To the overachievers

I promise to be by her side
Be her guiding star
In the thorny path
Of validations and aspirations

In hopelessness and despair
My dear unborn daughter
Be assured that you are loved
And will be loved forever.

First love

Rousing emotions and over pouring heart
Together it was the first of many walks

Maintaining distance and shying away
Blushing cheeks turning red

Walking down a lonely trail
We spoke in voices soft and frail

The first time we held hands
Felt like oceans brushing the sand

Emotionally immersed each strand of heart
Under the moonlight shining bright

Shadows followed us along
As if to each other we belong

The first love is magical
With a charm that leaves you whimsical

To be loved is a beautiful feeling
And to reciprocate love is pleasing.

www.ingramcontent.com/pod-product-compliance
Lightning Source LLC
La Vergne TN
LVHW011041200726
843509LV00011B/1329